Emu

or

Ostrich?

by Kirsten Chang

BLASTOFF! READERS

BELLWETHER MEDIA • MINNEAPOLIS, MN

Blastoff! Readers are carefully developed by literacy experts to build reading stamina and move students toward fluency by combining standards-based content with developmentally appropriate text.

Level 1 provides the most support through repetition of high-frequency words, light text, predictable sentence patterns, and strong visual support.

Level 2 offers early readers a bit more challenge through varied sentences, increased text load, and text-supportive special features.

Level 3 advances early-fluent readers toward fluency through increased text load, less reliance on photos, advancing concepts, longer sentences, and more complex special features.

★ **Blastoff! Universe**

Reading Level

Grade **K**

Grades **1–3**

Grade **4**

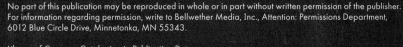

This edition first published in 2021 by Bellwether Media, Inc.

No part of this publication may be reproduced in whole or in part without written permission of the publisher. For information regarding permission, write to Bellwether Media, Inc., Attention: Permissions Department, 6012 Blue Circle Drive, Minnetonka, MN 55343.

Library of Congress Cataloging-in-Publication Data

Names: Chang, Kirsten, 1991- author.
Title: Emu or ostrich? / by Kirsten Chang.
Description: Minneapolis, MN : Bellwether Media, 2021. | Series: Blastoff readers : spotting differences | Includes bibliographical references and index. | Audience: Ages 5-8 | Audience: Grades K-1 | Summary: "Developed by literacy experts for students in kindergarten through grade three, this book introduces emus and ostriches to young readers through leveled text and related photos"-- Provided by publisher.
Identifiers: LCCN 2020035698 (print) | LCCN 2020035699 (ebook) | ISBN 9781644874035 (library binding) | ISBN 9781648340802 (ebook)
Subjects: LCSH: Emus--Juvenile literature. | Orstriches--Juvenile literature.
Classification: LCC QL696.C34 C43 2021 (print) | LCC QL696.C34 (ebook) | DDC 598.5/24--dc23
LC record available at https://lccn.loc.gov/2020035698
LC ebook record available at https://lccn.loc.gov/2020035699

Editor: Elizabeth Neuenfeldt   Designer: Laura Sowers

Printed in the United States of America, North Mankato, MN.

Table of Contents

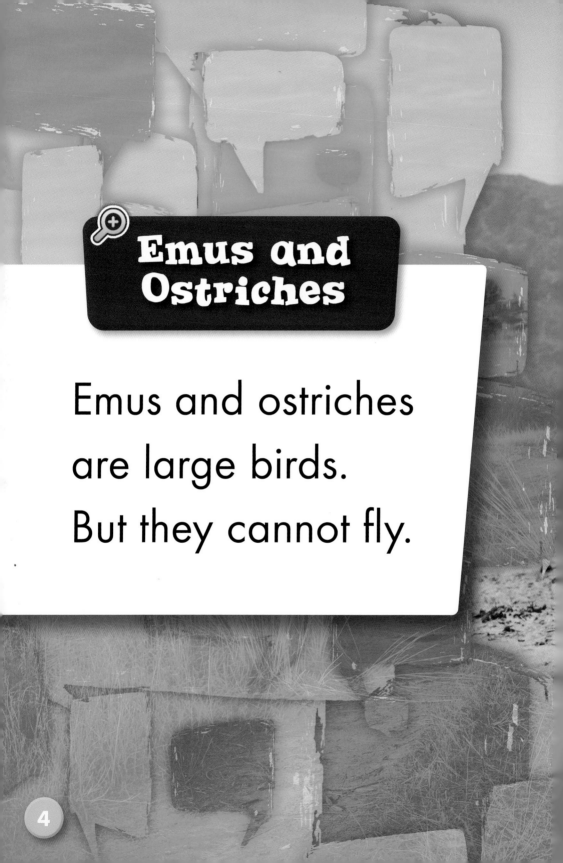

Emus and Ostriches

Emus and ostriches
are large birds.
But they cannot fly.

ostrich

5

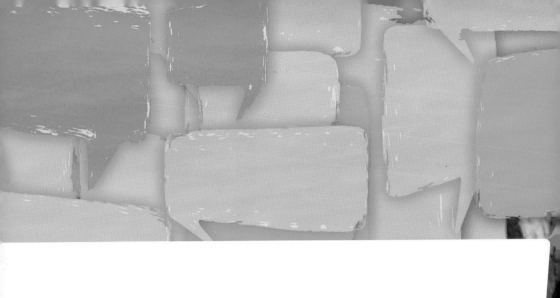

Both birds have
big eyes, long necks,
and long legs.
How are they different?

emu

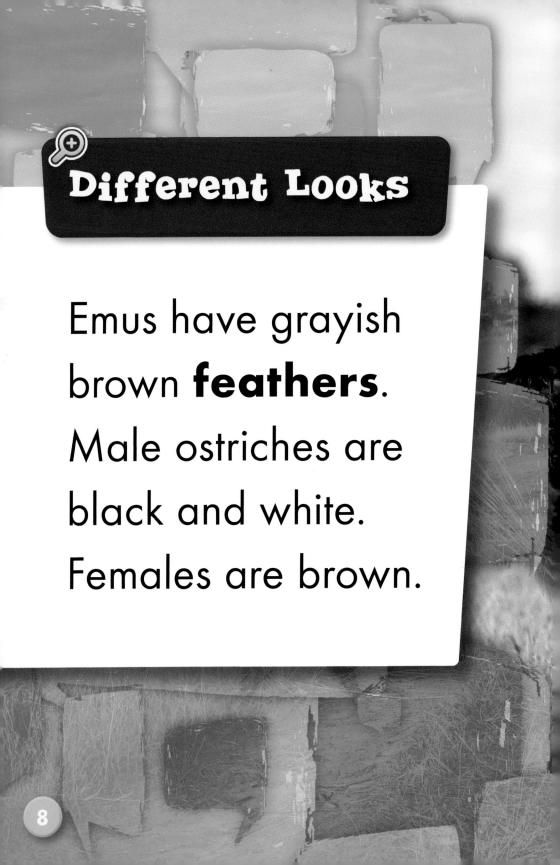

Emus have grayish brown **feathers**. Male ostriches are black and white. Females are brown.

feathers

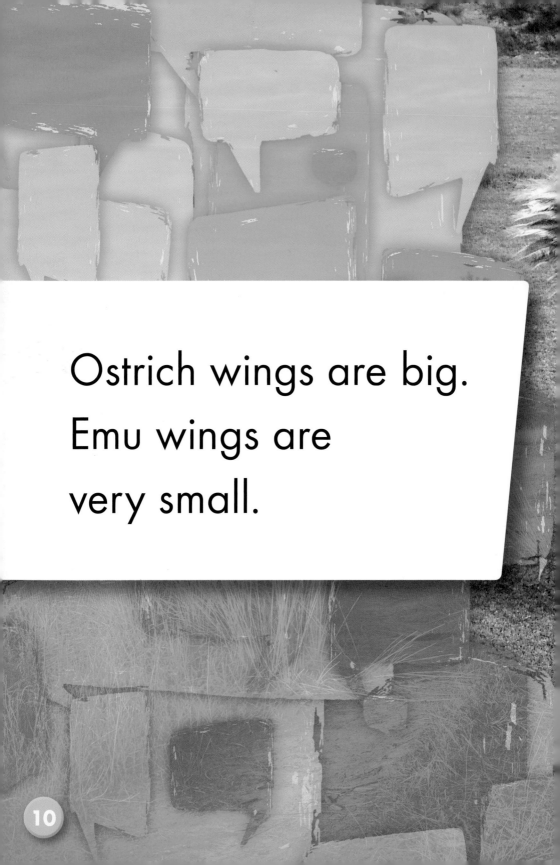

Ostrich wings are big.
Emu wings are
very small.

wing

Emu feet have
three toes. Ostrich feet
have two toes.
One toe has a **claw**!

← **claw**

Ostriches live in Africa.
Emus live in Australia.

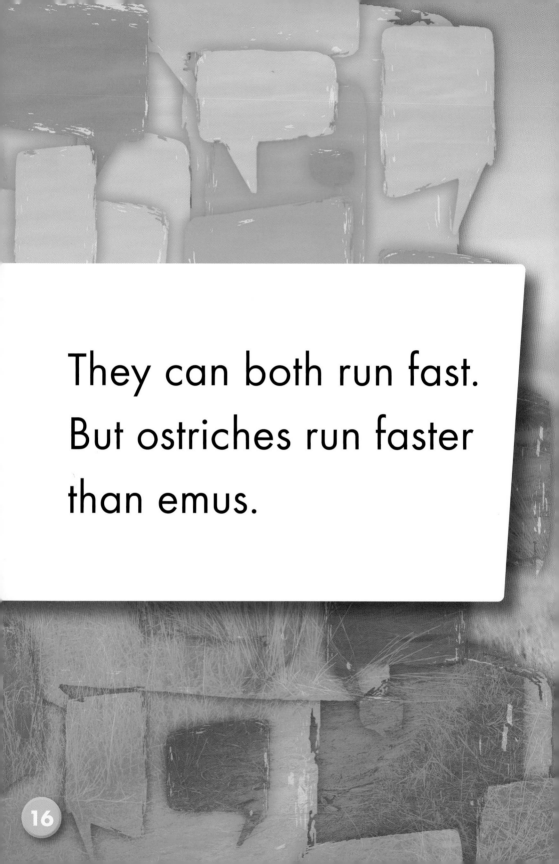

They can both run fast.
But ostriches run faster
than emus.

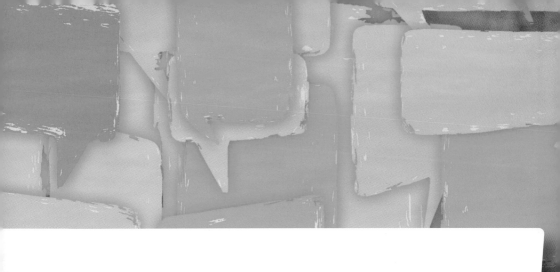

Emus must drink water daily. Ostriches can go days without water! Which bird is this?

Side by Side

grayish brown
feathers

small wings

three toes

Emu Differences

live in
Australia

must drink
water daily

run slower
than
ostriches

20

black and white or brown feathers

big wings

two toes, one with a claw

Ostrich Differences

live in Africa

can go days without water

run faster than emus

21

Glossary

claw

a sharp, curved nail on the toe of an animal

feathers

light, soft coverings on birds' bodies

To Learn More

AT THE LIBRARY

Emminizer, Theresa. *Awesome Ostriches.*
New York, N.Y.: PowerKids Press, 2021.

Hansen, Grace. *Emu.* Minneapolis, Minn.:
Abdo Kids Jumbo, 2020.

Nelson, Penelope S. *Ostriches.* Minneapolis,
Minn.: Jump! Inc., 2020.

ON THE WEB

FACTSURFER

Factsurfer.com gives you
a safe, fun way to find
more information.

1. Go to www.factsurfer.com.

2. Enter "emu or ostrich" into the search box
   and click Q.

3. Select your book cover to see a list
   of related content.

Index

The images in this book are reproduced through the courtesy of: Lukas_Vejrik, cover (emu), pp. 12-13; semue85, cover (ostrich); Sergei25, pp. 4-5; Neale Cousland, pp. 6-7; Art Konovalov, pp. 8-9; luispt, pp. 10-11; anne-tipodees, p. 11 (wings); Ekkachai, p. 13 (claw); SABPICS, pp. 14-15; Andrzej Kubik, pp. 16-17; Ken Griffiths, pp. 18-19; mariait, p. 20 (emu); Craig Dingle, p. 20 (drink); Samsonova Karina, p. 20 (run); Eric Isselee, p. 21 (ostrich); Chaithanya Krishnan, p. 21 (drink); paula french, p. 21 (run); Tuangtong Soraprasert, p. 22 (claw); Yana Vasileva, p. 22 (feathers).